One of the essential
elements

Richa

G000128274

water

Chris Mulhern

acorn book company

This edition published in the UK by
acorn book company
PO Box 191
Tadworth
Surrey. KT20 5YQ

email: sales@acornbook.co.uk

www.acornbook.co.uk

ISBN-0-9534205-0-7

British Library Cataloguing in Publication Data.
A catalogue record for this book is available from the British Library.

Trade distribution by Signature Book Representation Ltd. Manchester.
Tel: 0161-834-8767

© Chris Mulhern 1998
First published 1998

Illustrations by Katie Ellis
Computer Imaging by Alan Henning
Typeset by David Bird

poems for a pisces woman

CONTENTS

1. snowmelt

the   earth
hardfrozen
- sweet smell of woodsmoke

sacred   stones

glassy blue cold
plough - shine

rook flock flaps up - caw
cawing

then   settles...

there is a silence here

across the fresh cut
furrowed earth
a bonfire streams...

Winter :

a purring of sparrow-wings
leaving
the hedge

axe
knock
and   echo

logs   stacked
against   the   cold   flint
farmhouse   wall

crow
circles once
in   farewell

- but the sun has already set

a   bucket   clanks...

footsteps
and   the   farm
falls   silent

2. the dream

glowing logs, falling
to ash
in the grate...

the sound
of the embers
- glittering, quietly

through sleep, an owl calls
I picture its eyes
- blinking

where thins the veil
between the worlds

there I have held her
in my arms

a secret place...

she leads me
away

through the long grass
at dusk

the hem of her dress
wet with dew

I like the places you inhabit
the streams, the quiet places
the place of water
in the pool

when we get to the other side
- promise you'll come looking for me

3. cloud water

your   voice
receding

and   again,
receding

- was   that   you ?

Parting   the   curtains:

blackbird   calling
insistence   of   rain
falling   for   hours

outside

boy   with   a   big   umbrella
(ant   with   a   leaf)
late   for   something

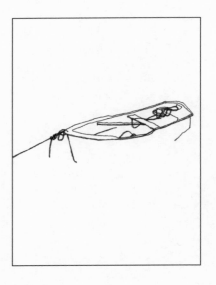

4. river journey

a spinning leaf
settles

on the cool clear
waters

and is bourne - bobbed away
downstream

the fishermen

bristling, quivering
procession of rods
 - laughter fading

silent fisherman
casts . . .
a still shadow

shoal
of brightfish
- passing

somewhere,
in   this   slow   dawn

is   a   ship
easing

out
of   the   harbour

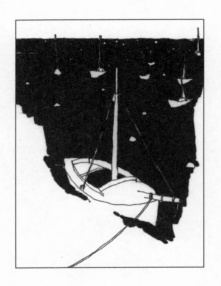

5. mussel shell blue

gull   coasts   in
low
its   reflection   rippling

dripping   rope   slack
hauled   in   hand
over   hand

smooth   hulls   lift
ropes   tauten
and   creak...

a string of lights
on mussel - shell blue

the wind
in the rope-tink masts

and beyond,

just the dark
lapping

sounds
of the sea

6. a small white cup

the sea, this morning
still blue,
and calm

the smell of coffee
from a small white
cup

her reading:
a teasing breeze, lifting
a few strands of hair

mid-morning:

wet bucket splash
drying off
on a doorstep

we bought oranges

and we sat on a bench
and ate them

sweet acid
- cush
of the juice

something of the river
in her eyes
- or was it the sea ?

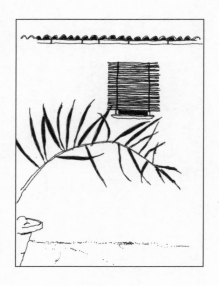

7. the quiet time

siesta hour:
at the rim of sleep
a canary, singing

in the curve
of your neck,
the scent of the sea

snuggling against your back

in my hand
the plump, softness
of your breast

in   the   courtyard

the   almond   tree
is   still

the   shadow
of   each   leaf

a   dark   fleck
on   the   white - washed   wall

till the early evening
breeze comes,
warmly rattling the blind

and the fountain spray, drifts
in the wind...

8. from a dream, waking

like some kind of sea-wrack
washed up
in each other's arms

tea time:

stuffing a stale-dry crust
through the bars
of the canary's cage

white-washed walls
with flowers,
dripping

      - magenta

9.   dusty track

dusty   track
with   a   few   good
kickable   stones

crow
pecking at something
baked onto the road

warm breeze
across the valley
gentle music of goat bells,

a rugged kind of beauty

this red earth
dusty with rocks
and the dry scent of sage

hoe-flash
high
on a hillside

sun dark forearms
smooth hoe handle,
  - wood-shiny

weathered he was
like the bark of a tree

weathered by love,
and indifference

a tree weathered
by a thousand suns

goat hoof hit
scattering
silence

10. dry land

hazy

summer's evening stillness
 - looking back
the way we have come

golden stalks of hay, strewn
over the earth
after harvest

the air heavy
with scent
and thunder coming

she looks up at the sky
and I see the clouds, passing
her eyes

heard the rain
on the dead bracken
long before I felt a drop

water:
your seeking for dryness, for thirst
for all that is arid in me

Thank you to everyone who helped bring this book into being - especially Pam, Dave, Katie, Al, Rob and Nick.

also by Chris Mulhern:

cloud blunt moon

a sequence of poems
based on the phases of the moon.
Illustrated with charcoal sketches.

order direct from:

acorn book company
PO Box 191
Tadworth
Surrey. KT20 5YQ
email: sales@acornbook.co.uk
or your local bookshop.

acorn

acorn book company is an independent
publisher of small, high quality editions.

We also operate a mail order web-site
specialising in haiku and minimalist poetry.

For more information
please visit us at:
www.acornbook.co.uk